FINGERPICK

BROADWAY FAVORITES

ISBN 978-1-4234-1656-2

Visit Hal Leonard Online at www.halleonard.com

HAL•LEONARD®
CORPORATION
7777 W. BLUEMOUND RD. P.O. BOX 13819 MILWAUKEE, WI 53213

FINGERPICKING
BROADWAY FAVORITES

INTRODUCTION TO FINGERSTYLE GUITAR

Fingerstyle (a.k.a. fingerpicking) is a guitar technique that means you literally pick the strings with your right-hand fingers and thumb. This contrasts with the conventional technique of strumming and playing single notes with a pick (a.k.a. flatpicking). For fingerpicking, you can use any type of guitar: acoustic steel-string, nylon-string classical, or electric.

THE RIGHT HAND

The most common right-hand position is shown here.

Use a high wrist; arch your palm as if you were holding a ping-pong ball. Keep the thumb outside and away from the fingers, and let the fingers do the work rather than lifting your whole hand.

The thumb generally plucks the bottom strings with downstrokes on the left side of the thumb and thumbnail. The other fingers pluck the higher strings using upstokes with the fleshy tip of the fingers and fingernails. The thumb and fingers should pluck one string per stroke and not brush over several strings.

Another picking option you may choose to use is called hybrid picking (a.k.a. plectrum-style fingerpicking). Here, the pick is usually held between the thumb and first finger, and the three remaining fingers are assigned to pluck the higher strings.

THE LEFT HAND

The left-hand fingers are numbered 1 though 4.

Be sure to keep your fingers arched, with each joint bent; if they flatten out across the strings, they will deaden the sound when you fingerpick. As a general rule, let the strings ring as long as possible when playing fingerstyle.

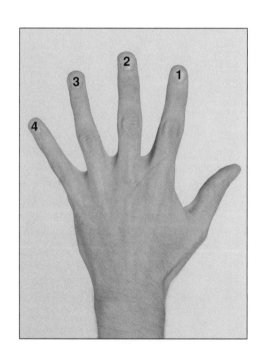

Cabaret
from the Musical CABARET
Words by Fred Ebb
Music by John Kander

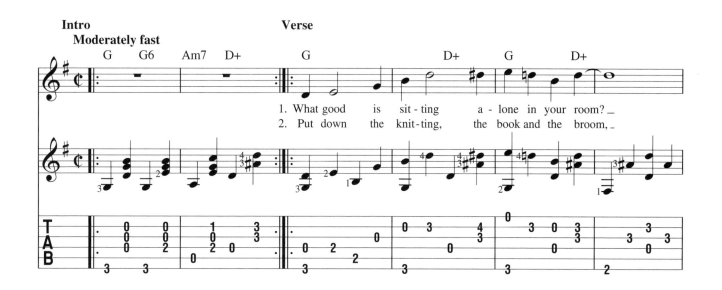

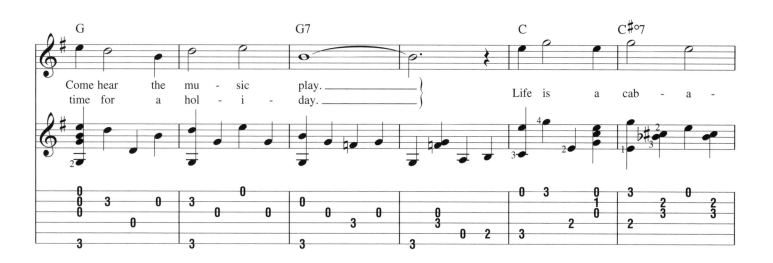

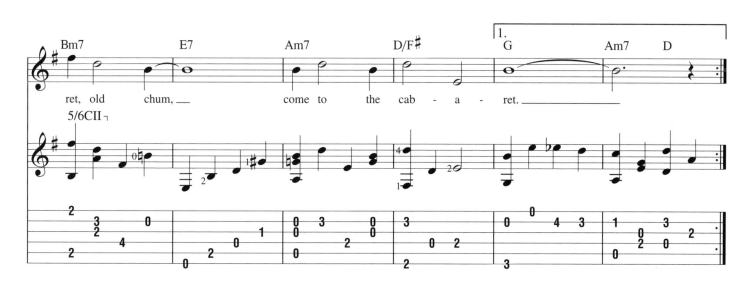

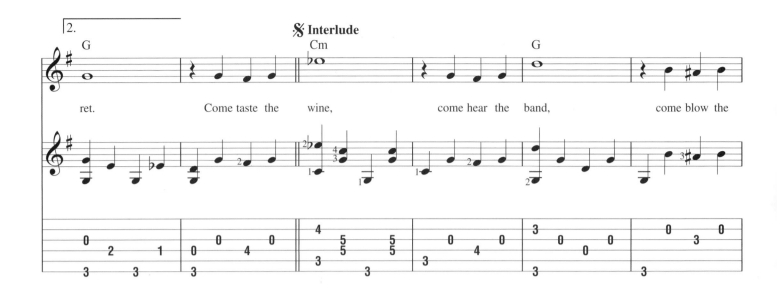

Come taste the wine, come hear the band, come blow the

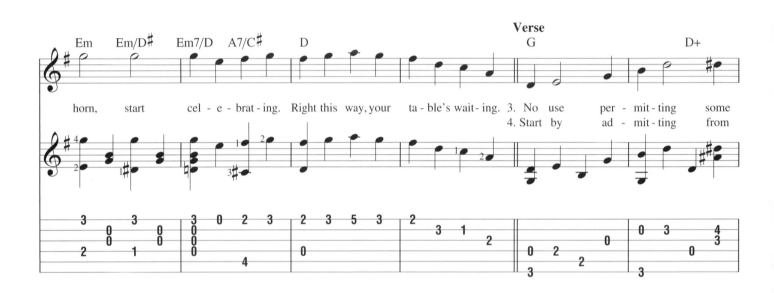

horn, start cel - e - brat - ing. Right this way, your ta - ble's wait - ing. 3. No use per - mit - ting some
4. Start by ad - mit - ting from

proph - et of doom ___ to wipe ev - 'ry smile a - way. ___
cra - dle to tomb ___ is - n't that long a stay. ___

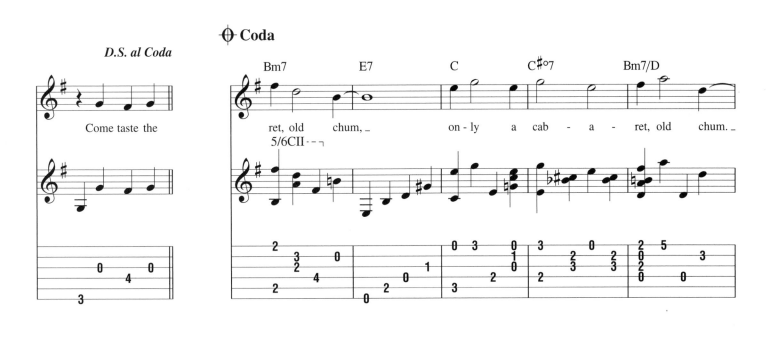

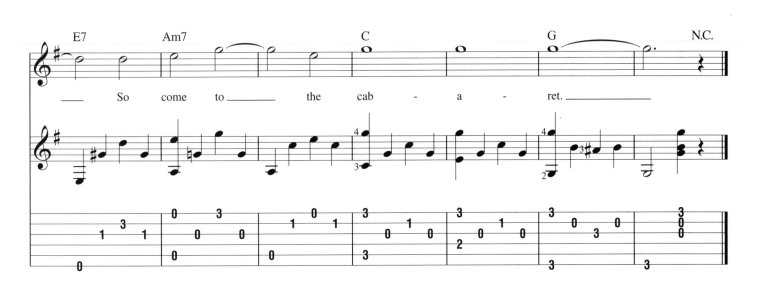

Big Spender

from SWEET CHARITY

Music by Cy Coleman
Lyrics by Dorothy Fields

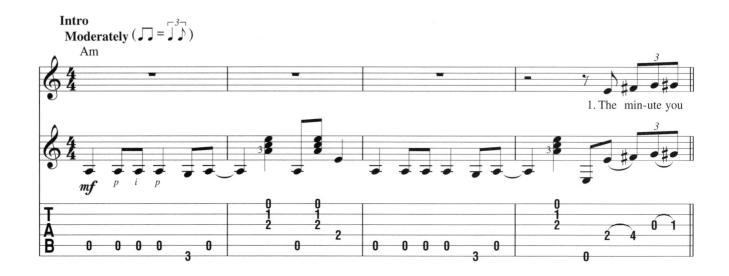

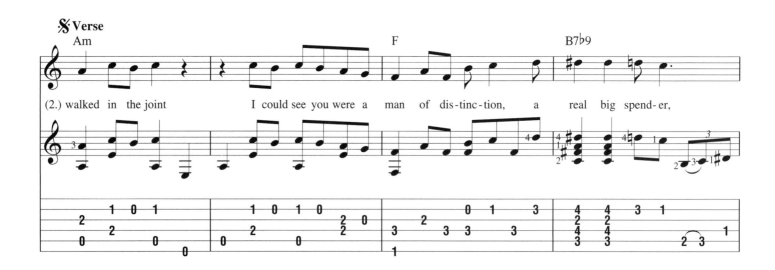

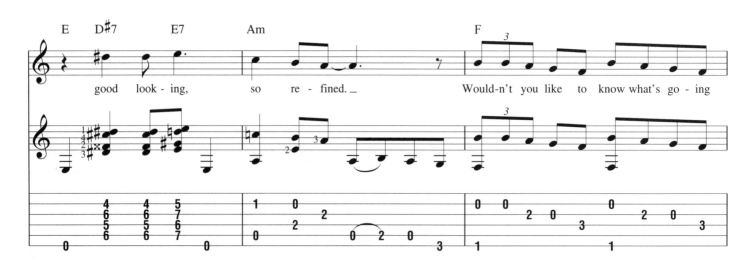

D.S. al Coda

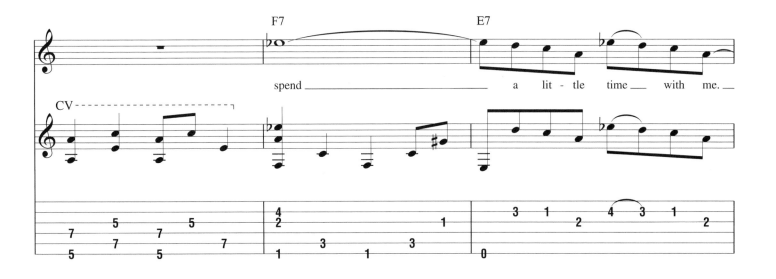

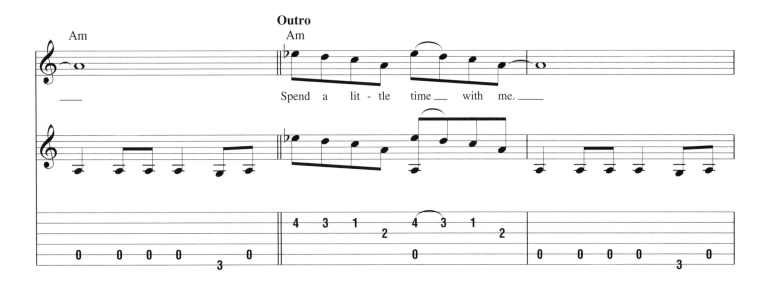

Falling in Love with Love

from THE BOYS FROM SYRACUSE

Words by Lorenz Hart
Music by Richard Rodgers

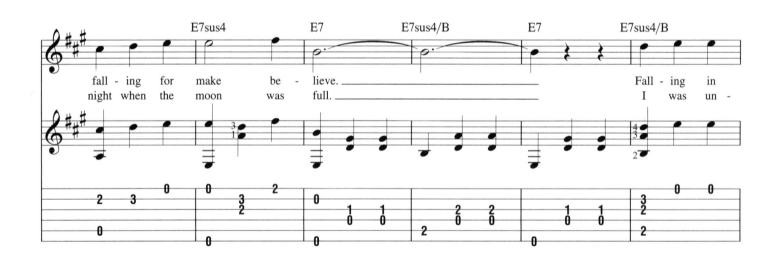

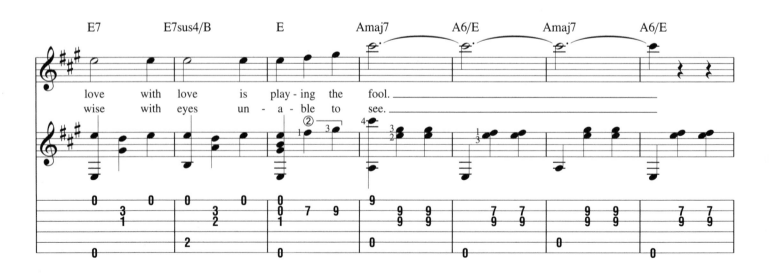

I'll Be Seeing You

from RIGHT THIS WAY

Written by Irving Kahal and Sammy Fain

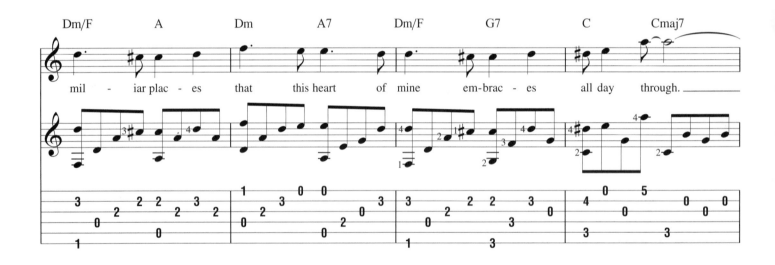

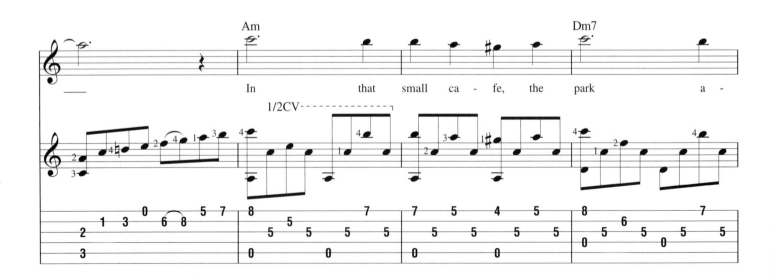

cross the way, the chil - dren's car - ou - sel, __ the chest-nut trees, __ the

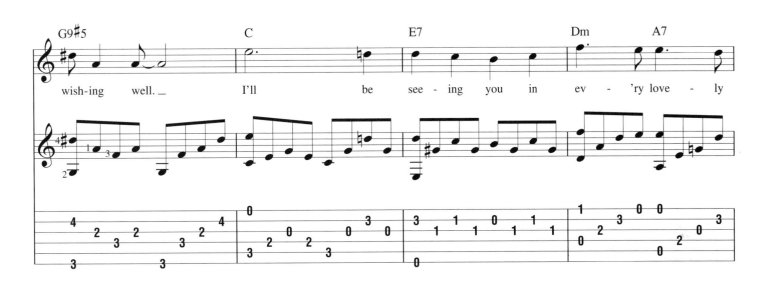

wish-ing well. __ I'll be see - ing you in ev - 'ry love - ly

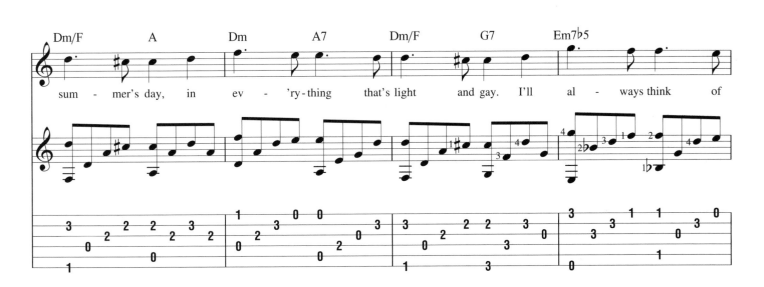

sum - mer's day, in ev - 'ry-thing that's light and gay. I'll al - ways think of

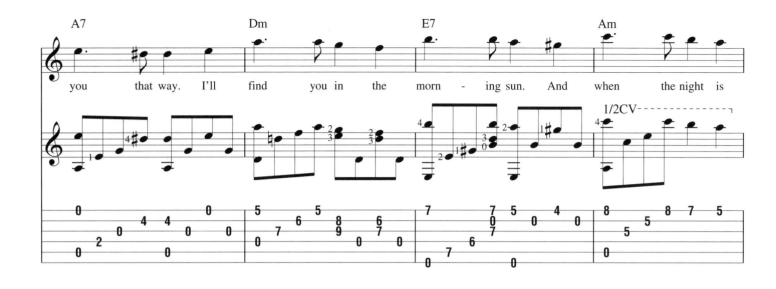

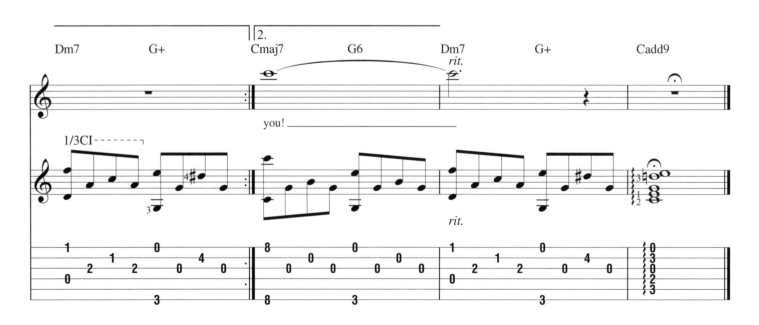

Manhattan

from the Broadway Musical THE GARRICK GAIETIES

Words by Lorenz Hart
Music by Richard Rodgers

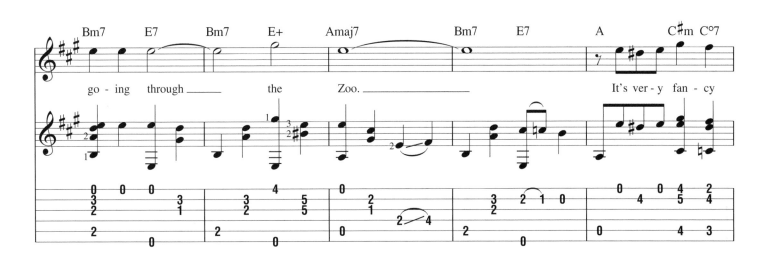

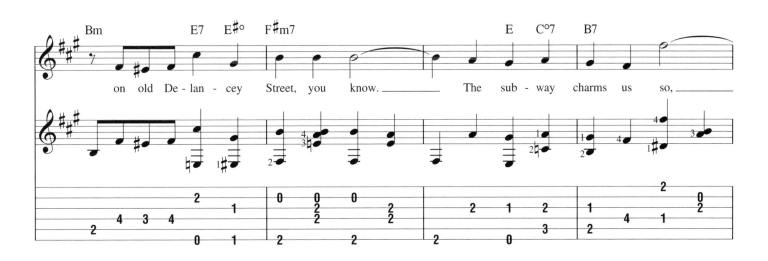

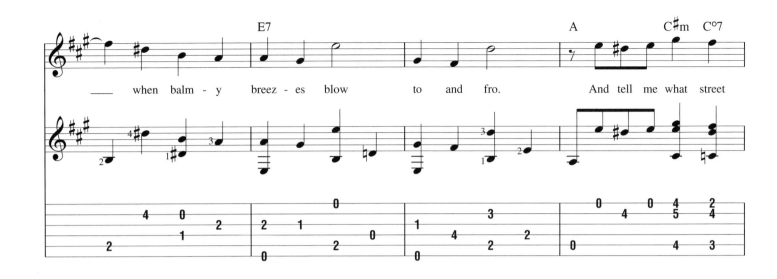

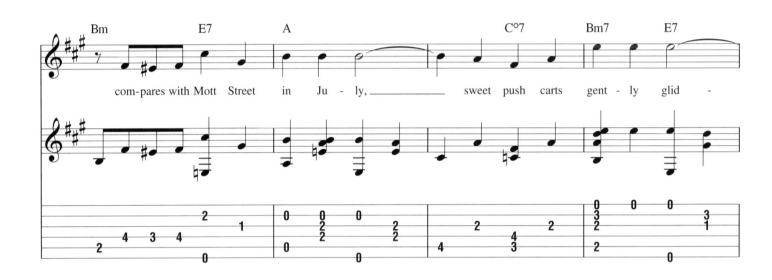

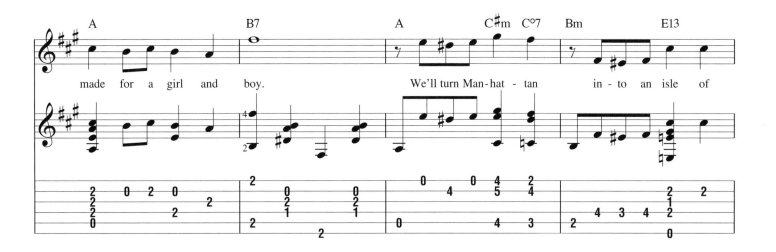

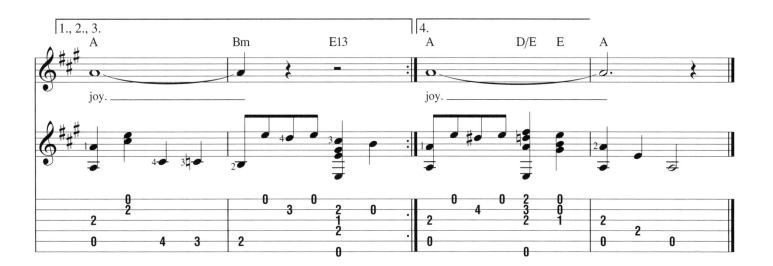

Additional Lyrics

2. We'll go to Greenwich where modern men itch to be free,
   And Bowling Green you'll see with me.
   We'll bathe at Brighton, the fish you'll frighten when you're in.
   Your bathing suit so thin will make the shellfish grin fin to fin.
   I'd like to take a sail on Jamaica Bay with you
   And fair Canarsie's lakes we'll view.
   The city's bustle cannot destroy
   The dreams of a girl and boy.
   We'll turn Manhattan into an isle of joy.

3. We'll go to Yonkers where true love conquers in the wilds,
   And starve together, dear, in Childs.
   We'll go to Coney and eat baloney on a roll.
   In Central Park we'll stroll where our first kisses we stole, soul to soul.
   Our future babies we'll take to Abie's Irish Rose.
   I hope they'll live to see it close.
   The city's clamor can never spoil
   The dreams of a boy and goil.
   We'll turn Manhattan into an isle of joy.

4. We'll have Manhattan, the Bronx and Staten Island too.
   We'll try to cross Fifth Avenue.
   As black as onyx we'll find the Bronnix Park Express.
   Our Flatbush flat, I guess, will be a great success, more or less.
   A short vacation on Inspiration Point we'll spend,
   And in the station house we'll end.
   But civic virtue cannot destroy
   The dreams of a girl and boy.
   We'll turn Manhattan into an isle of joy.

If I Were a Rich Man

from the Musical FIDDLER ON THE ROOF

Words by Sheldon Harnick
Music by Jerry Bock

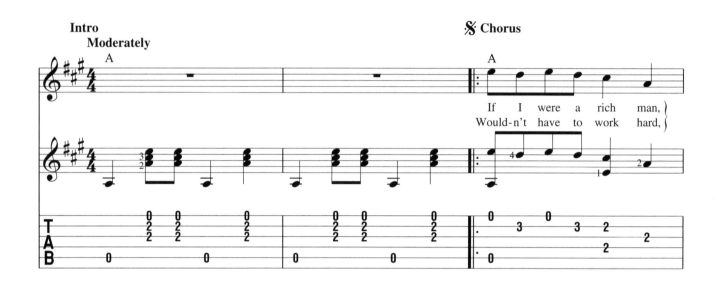

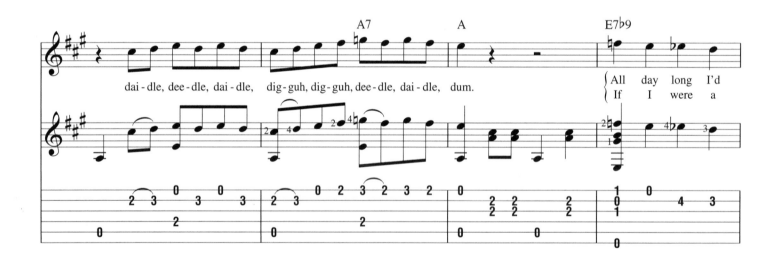

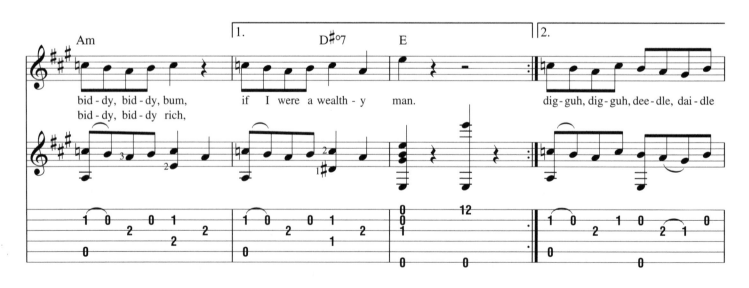

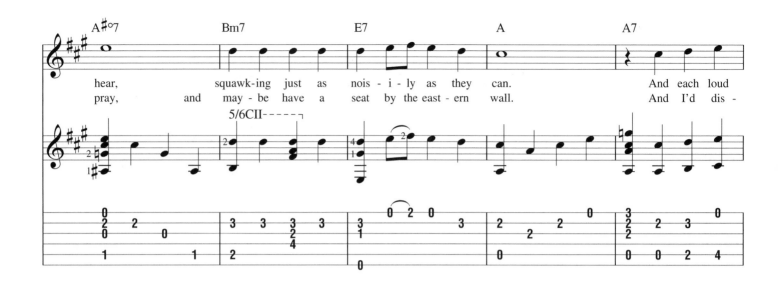

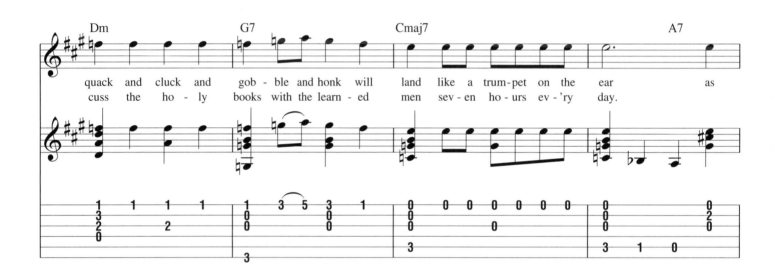

Outro-Chorus

If I were a rich man, }
Would-n't have to work hard, }
dai-dle, dee-dle, dai-dle, dig-guh, dig-guh, dee-dle, dai-dle, dum.

{ All day long I'd
{ Lord, who made the
bid-dy, bid-dy, bum,
li-on and the lamb,
if I were a wealth-y man.
You de-cree I

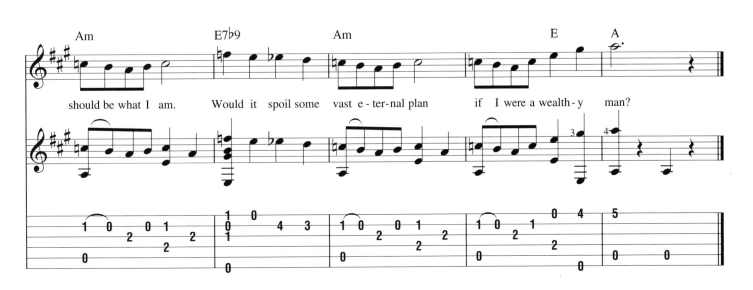

should be what I am. Would it spoil some vast e-ter-nal plan if I were a wealth-y man?

Oklahoma

from OKLAHOMA!

Lyrics by Oscar Hammerstein II
Music by Richard Rodgers

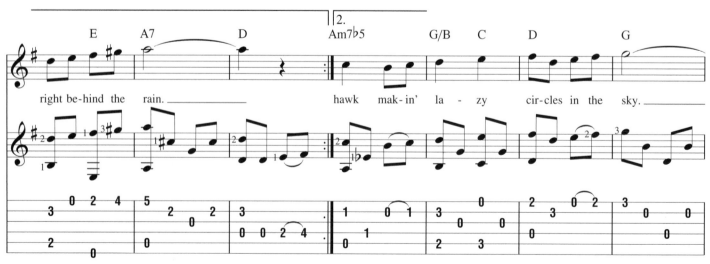

One

from A CHORUS LINE

Music by Marvin Hamlisch
Lyric by Edward Kleban

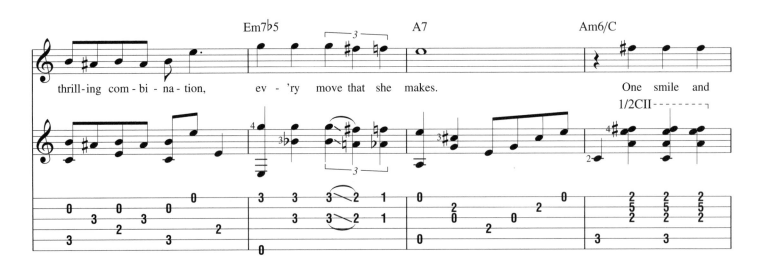

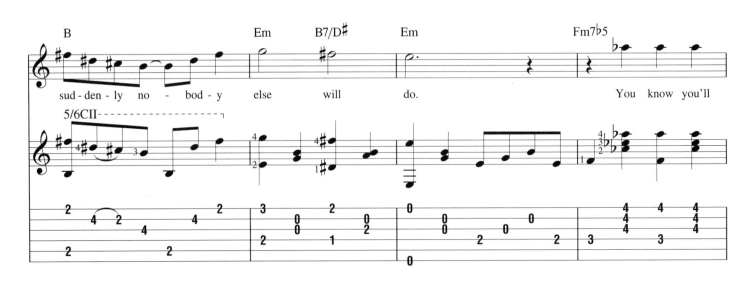

My Cup Runneth Over

from I DO! I DO!

Words by Tom Jones
Music by Harvey Schmidt

Additional Lyrics

2. Sometimes in the evening when you do not see,
   I study the small things you do constantly.
   I memorize moments that I'm fondest of.
   My cup runneth over with love.

3. In only a moment we both will be old.
   We won't even notice the world turning cold.
   And so in this moment with sunlight above,
   My cup runneth over with love, with love.

Seasons of Love

from RENT

Words and Music by Jonathan Larson

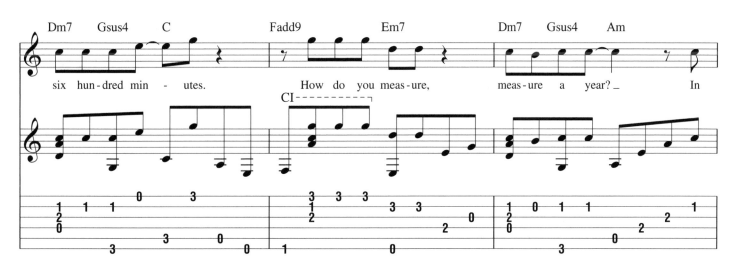

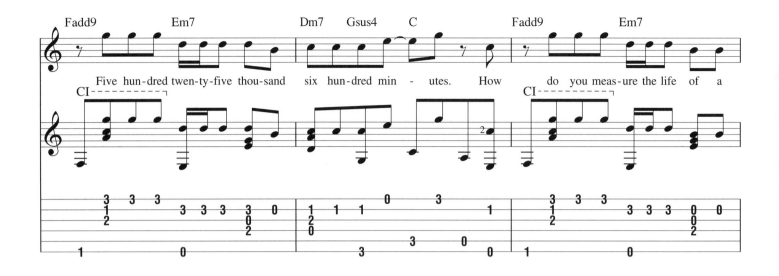

Five hun-dred twen-ty-five thou-sand six hun-dred min - utes. How do you meas-ure the life of a

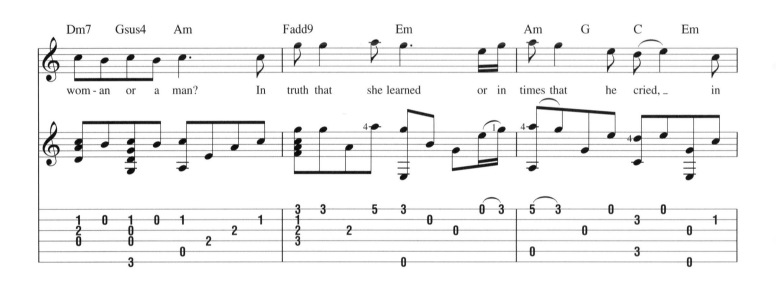

wom-an or a man? In truth that she learned or in times that he cried, _ in

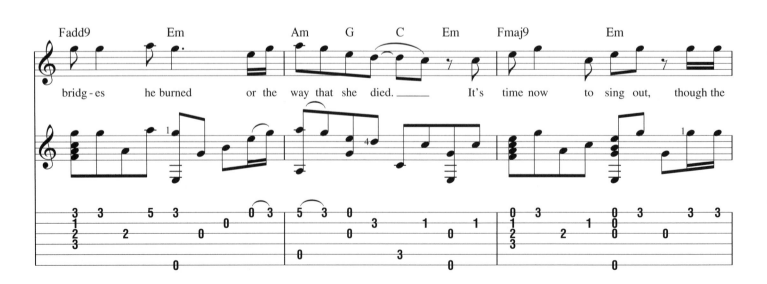

bridg-es he burned or the way that she died. _____ It's time now to sing out, though the

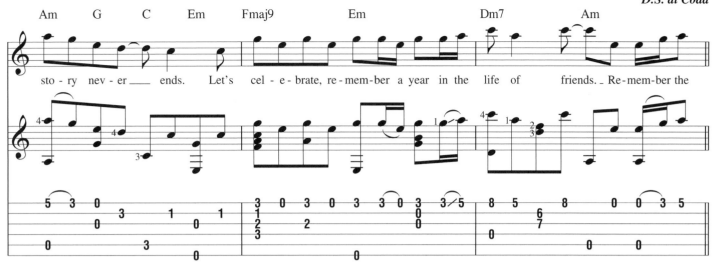

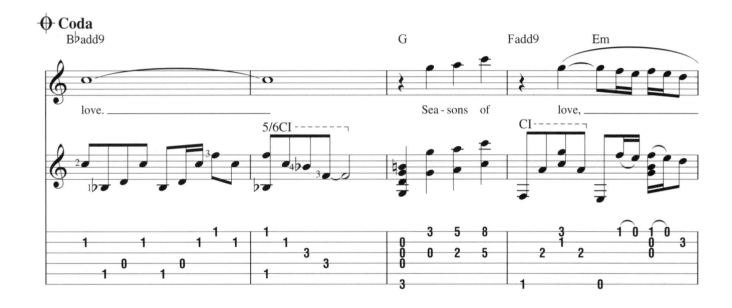

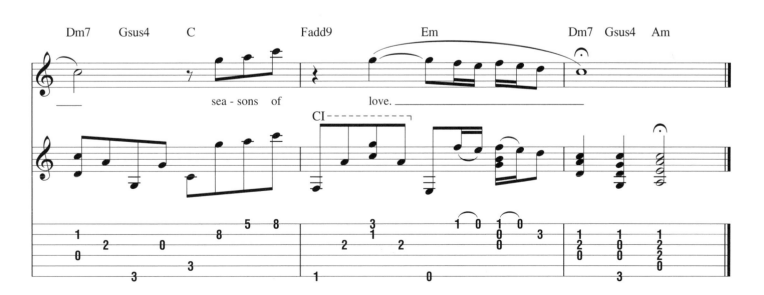

Smoke Gets in Your Eyes

from ROBERTA

Words by Otto Harbach
Music by Jerome Kern

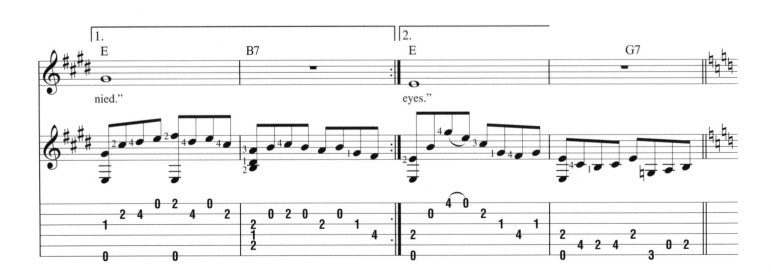

Bridge

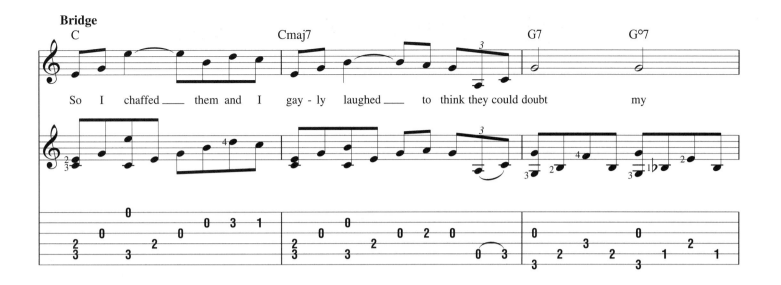

So I chaffed ___ them and I gay - ly laughed ___ to think they could doubt my

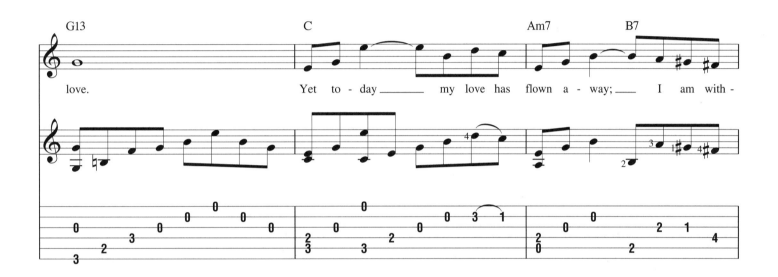

love. Yet to - day ___ my love has flown a - way; ___ I am with -

D.C. al Coda

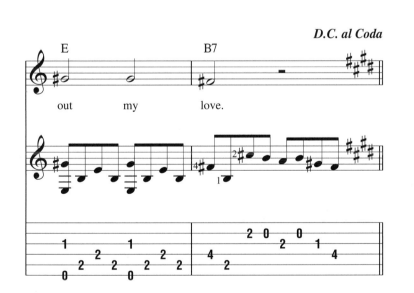

out my love.

⊕ **Coda**

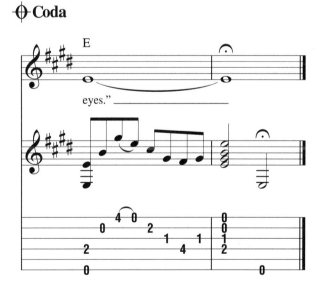

eyes." _____

Additional Lyrics

2. They said, "Someday you'll find
   All who love are blind.
   When your heart's on fire, you must realize,
   Smoke gets in your eyes."

3. Now laughing friends deride
   Tears I cannot hide,
   So I smile and say, "When a lovely flame dies,
   Smoke gets in your eyes."

What'll I Do?

from MUSIC BOX REVUE OF 1924

Words and Music by Irving Berlin

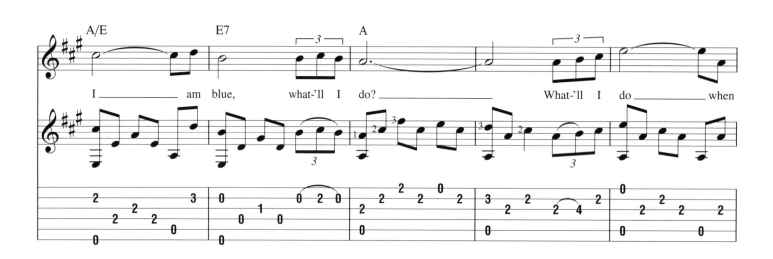

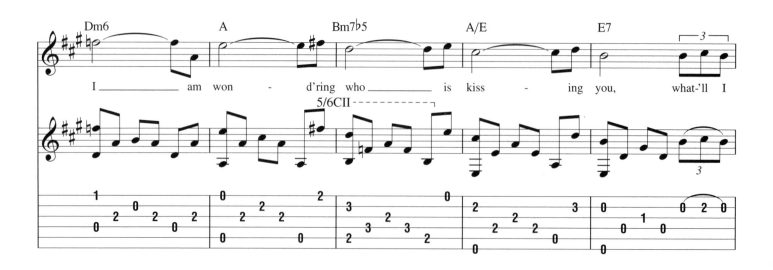

Where Is Love?

from the Broadway Musical OLIVER!

Words and Music by Lionel Bart

Verse
Slowly

1. Where _____ is love? Does it fall from skies a -
2. Where _____ is she who I close my eyes to

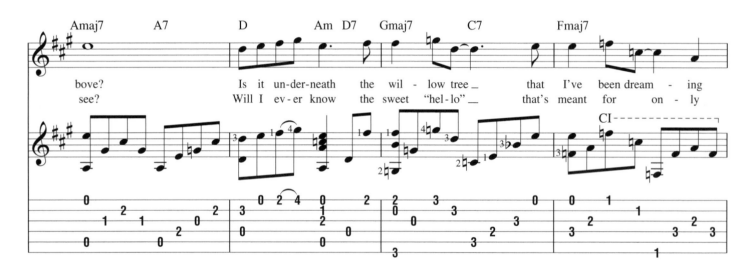

bove? Is it un-der-neath the wil - low tree _ that I've been dream - ing
see? Will I ev-er know the sweet "hel-lo" _ that's meant for on - ly

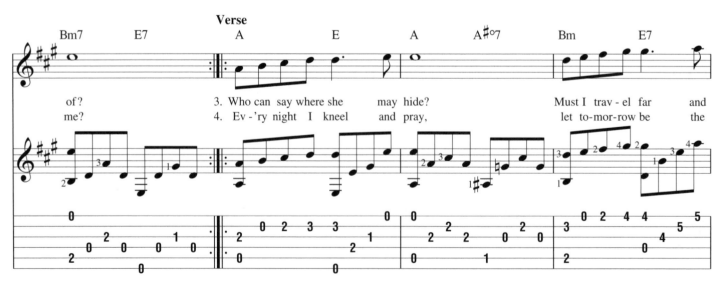

of? Must I trav-el far and
me? let to-mor-row be the

3. Who can say where she may hide?
4. Ev - 'ry night I kneel and pray,

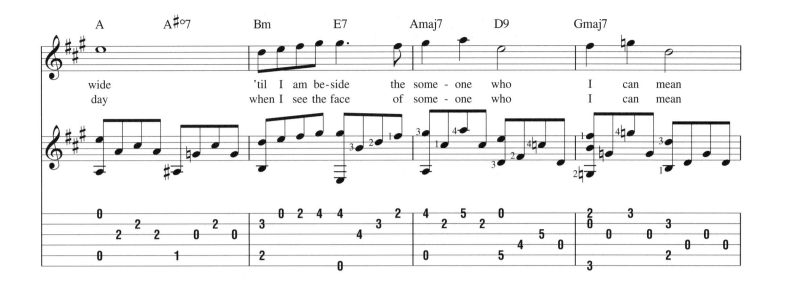

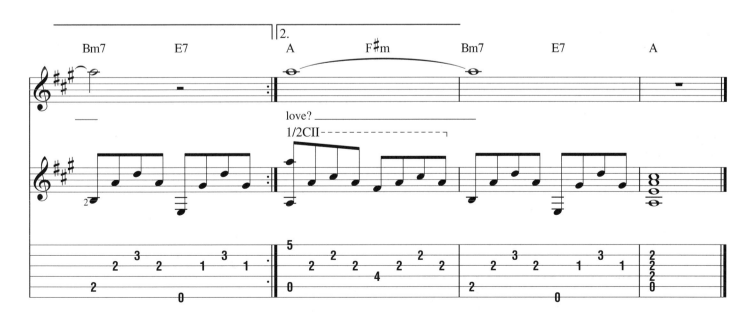

Thank Heaven for Little Girls

from GIGI

Words by Alan Jay Lerner
Music by Frederick Loewe

Drop D tuning:
(low to high) D-A-D-G-B-E

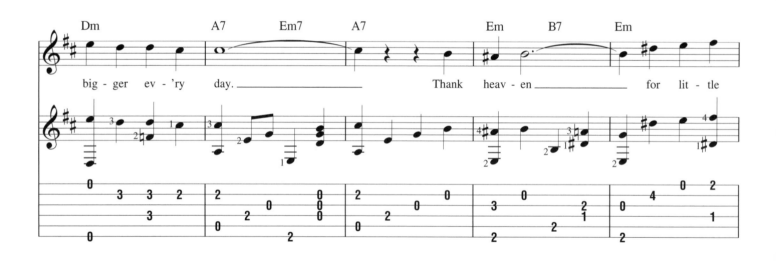

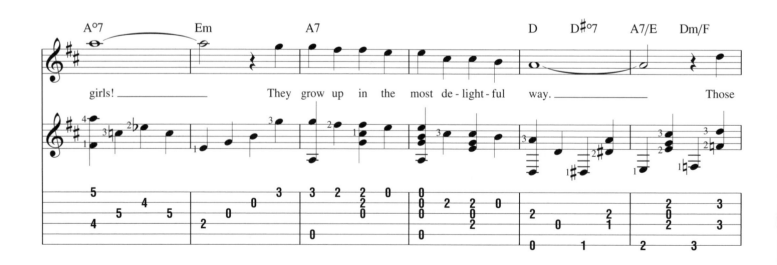

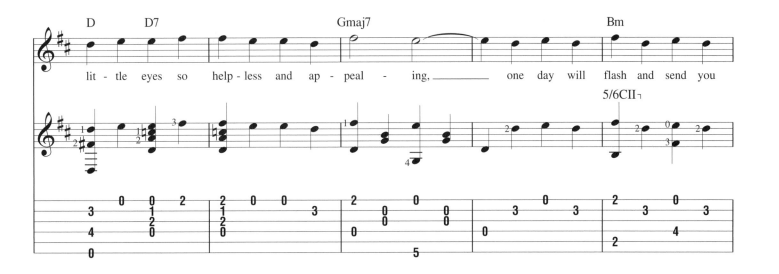

lit - tle eyes so help - less and ap - peal - ing, _____ one day will flash and send you

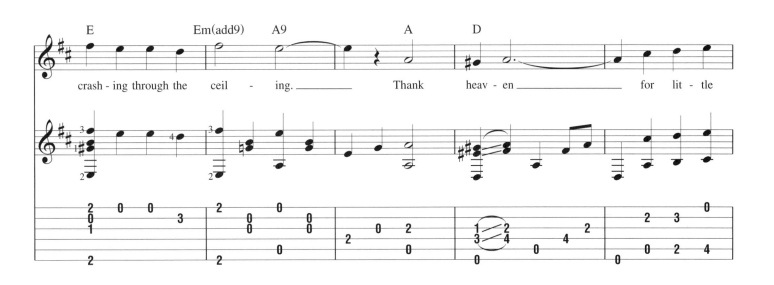

crash - ing through the ceil - ing. _____ Thank heav - en _____ for lit - tle

girls, _____ thank heav - en for them all no mat - ter where, no mat - ter who. With-

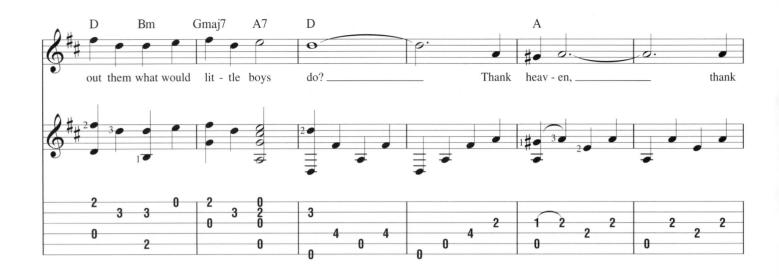

out them what would lit - tle boys do? _____ Thank heav - en, _____ thank

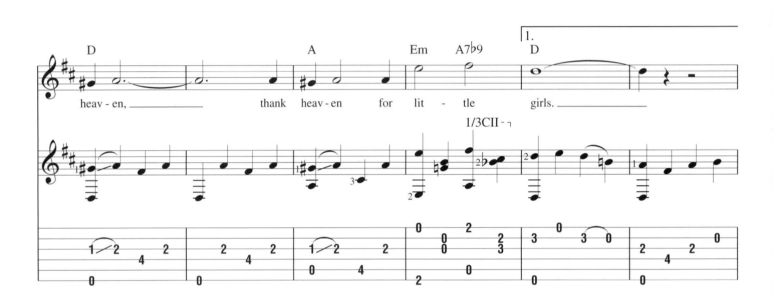

heav - en, _____ thank heav - en for lit - tle girls. _____

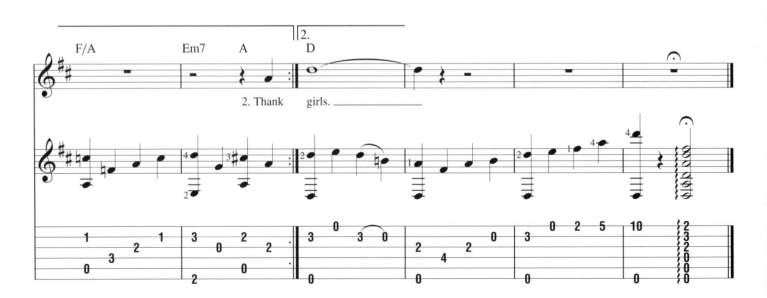

2. Thank girls. _____

Who Can I Turn To
(When Nobody Needs Me)

from THE ROAR OF THE GREASEPAINT - THE SMELL OF THE CROWD
Words and Music by Leslie Bricusse and Anthony Newley

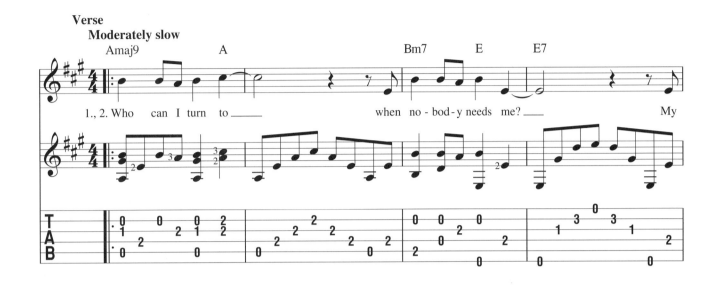

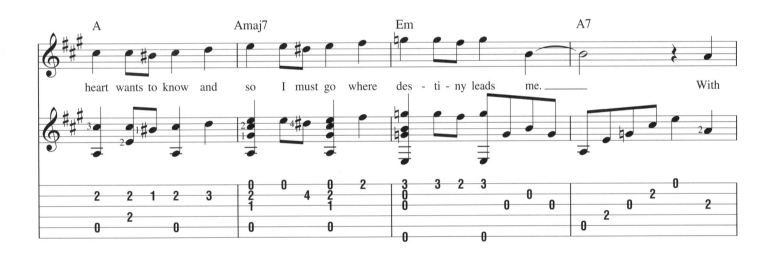

go on my way, and af - ter the day, the dark - ness will hide me. _____ And

may - be to - mor - row _____ I'll find what I'm af - ter. _____ I'll

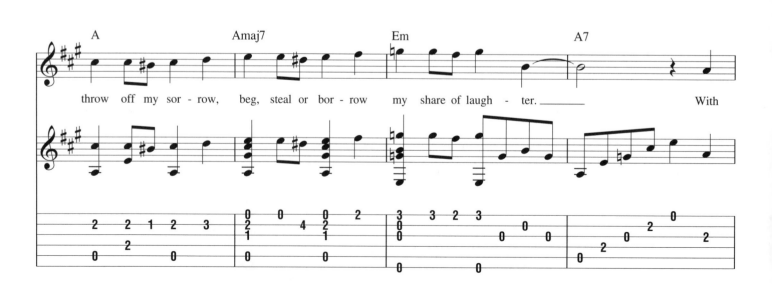

throw off my sor - row, beg, steal or bor - row my share of laugh - ter. _____ With

you I could learn to,___ with you on a new day,___ but

who can I turn to if you turn a - way? ___

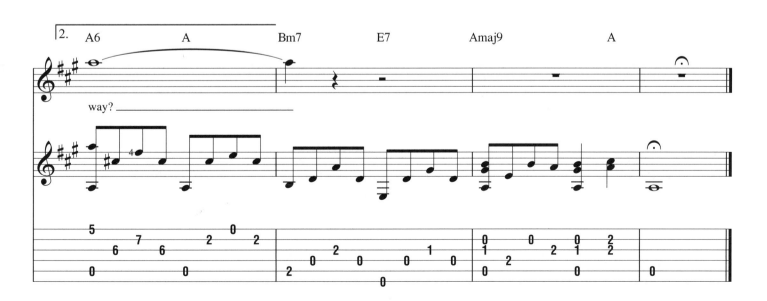

way? ___

FINGERPICKING
GUITAR BOOKS

Hone your fingerpicking skills with these great songbooks featuring solo guitar arrangements in standard notation and tablature. The arrangements in these books are carefully written for intermediate-level guitarists. Each song combines melody and harmony in one superb guitar fingerpicking arrangement. Each book also includes an introduction to basic fingerstyle guitar.

FINGERPICKING ACOUSTIC

15 songs: Behind Blue Eyes • Best of My Love • Blowin' in the Wind • The Boxer • Dust in the Wind • Helplessly Hoping • Hey Jude • In My Life • Learning to Fly • Leaving on a Jet Plane • Tears in Heaven • Time in a Bottle • You've Got a Friend • and more.
00699614 ....$8.95

FINGERPICKING ACOUSTIC ROCK

15 songs: American Pie • Bridge over Troubled Water • Every Rose Has Its Thorn • Knockin' on Heaven's Door • Landslide • More Than Words • Norwegian Wood (This Bird Has Flown) • Suite: Judy Blue Eyes • Wanted Dead or Alive • and more.
00699764 ....$7.95

FINGERPICKING BACH

12 masterpieces from J.S. Bach: Air on the G String • Bourrée in E Minor • Jesu, Joy of Man's Desiring • Little Prelude No. 2 in C Major • Minuet in G • Prelude in C Major • Quia Respexit • Sheep May Safely Graze • and more.
00699793 ....$8.95

FINGERPICKING BALLADS

15 songs: Against All Odds • (Everything I Do) I Do It for You • Fields of Gold • Have I Told You Lately • It's All Coming Back to Me Now • Looks Like We Made It • Rainy Days and Mondays • Say You, Say Me • She's Got a Way • Your Song • and more.
00699717 ....$8.95

FINGERPICKING BEATLES

30 songs including: All You Need Is Love • And I Love Her • Can't Buy Me Love • Hey Jude • In My Life • Lady Madonna • Let It Be • Love Me Do • Michelle • Nowhere Man • Please Please Me • Something • Ticket to Ride • Yellow Submarine • Yesterday • and more.
00699049 ....$19.95

FINGERPICKING CHILDREN'S SONGS

15 songs: Any Dream Will Do • Do-Re-Mi • It's a Small World • Linus and Lucy • The Muppet Show Theme • Puff the Magic Dragon • The Rainbow Connection • Sesame Street Theme • Winnie the Pooh • Zip-A-Dee-Doo-Dah • and more.
00699712 ....$8.95

FINGERPICKING CHRISTMAS

20 classic carols: Away in a Manger • Deck the Hall • The First Noel • God Rest Ye, Merry Gentlemen • Hark! The Herald Angels Sing • It Came Upon the Midnight Clear • Jingle Bells • O Little Town of Bethlehem • Silent Night • What Child Is This • and more.
00699599 ....$7.95

FINGERPICKING CLASSICAL

15 songs: Ave Maria • Bourée in E Minor • Canon in D • Eine Kleine Nachtmusik • Für Elise • Habanera • Minuet in G Major (Bach) • Minuet in G Major (Beethoven) • New World Symphony • Pomp and Circumstance • and more.
00699620 ....$8.95

FOR MORE INFORMATION, SEE YOUR LOCAL MUSIC DEALER,
OR WRITE TO:

HAL•LEONARD®
CORPORATION
7777 W. BLUEMOUND RD. P.O. BOX 13819 MILWAUKEE, WI 53213

Visit Hal Leonard online at www.halleonard.com

FINGERPICKING COUNTRY

17 classic favorites: Always on My Mind • By the Time I Get to Phoenix • Could I Have This Dance • Crazy • Green Green Grass of Home • He Stopped Loving Her Today • I Walk the Line • King of the Road • Tennessee Waltz • You Are My Sunshine • and more.
00699687 ....$8.95

FINGERPICKING DISNEY

15 songs: The Bare Necessities • Beauty and the Beast • Can You Feel the Love Tonight • Colors of the Wind • Go the Distance • If I Didn't Have You • Look Through My Eyes • Reflection • Under the Sea • A Whole New World • You'll Be in My Heart • and more.
00699711 ....$9.95

FINGERPICKING HYMNS

15 songs: Amazing Grace • Beneath the Cross of Jesus • Come, Thou Fount of Every Blessing • For the Beauty of the Earth • I've Got Peace like a River • Jacob's Ladder • A Mighty Fortress Is Our God • Rock of Ages • and more.
00699688 ....$8.95

FINGERPICKING ANDREW LLOYD WEBBER

14 songs: All I Ask of You • Don't Cry for Me Argentina • Memory • The Music of the Night • With One Look • more.
00699839 ....$7.95

FINGERPICKING MOZART

15 of Mozart's timeless compositions: Ave Verum • Eine Kleine Nachtmusik • Laudate Dominum • Minuet in G Major, K. 1 • Piano Concerto No. 21 in C Major • Piano Sonata in A • Piano Sonata in C • Rondo in C Major • and more.
00699794 ....$8.95

FINGERPICKING POP

Includes 15 songs: Can You Feel the Love Tonight • Don't Know Why • Endless Love • Imagine • Let It Be • My Cherie Amour • My Heart Will Go On • Piano Man • Stand by Me • We've Only Just Begun • Wonderful Tonight • and more.
00699615 ....$8.95

FINGERPICKING PRAISE

15 songs: Above All • Breathe • Draw Me Close • Great Is the Lord • He Is Exalted • Jesus, Name Above All Names • Oh Lord, You're Beautiful • Open the Eyes of My Heart • Shine, Jesus, Shine • Shout to the Lord • You Are My King • and more.
00699714 ....$8.95

FINGERPICKING ROCK

15 songs: Abracadabra • Brown Eyed Girl • Crocodile Rock • Free Bird • The House of the Rising Sun • I Want You to Want Me • Livin' on a Prayer • Maggie May • Rhiannon • Still the Same • When the Children Cry • and more.
00699716 ....$8.95

FINGERPICKING STANDARDS

17 fantastic songs: Can't Help Falling in Love • Fly Me to the Moon • Georgia on My Mind • I Just Called to Say I Love You • Just the Way You Are • Misty • Moon River • Unchained Melody • What a Wonderful World • When I Fall in Love • Yesterday • and more.
00699613 ....$8.95

FINGERPICKING WEDDING

15 tunes for the big day: Beautiful in My Eyes • Don't Know Much • Endless Love • Grow Old with Me • In My Life • The Lord's Prayer • This Is the Day (A Wedding Song) • We've Only Just Begun • Wedding Processional • You and I • and more.
00699637 ....$8.95

FINGERPICKING YULETIDE

16 holiday favorites: Blue Christmas • The Christmas Song • Frosty the Snow Man • A Holly Jolly Christmas • I'll Be Home for Christmas • Jingle-Bell Rock • Let It Snow! Let It Snow! Let It Snow! • Merry Christmas, Darling • Rudolph the Red-Nosed Reindeer • and more.
00699654 ....$8.95

Prices, contents and availability subject to change without notice.

PLAY THE CLASSICS

JAZZ FOLIOS FOR GUITARISTS

BEST OF JAZZ GUITAR

by Wolf Marshall • Signature Licks

In this book/CD pack, Wolf Marshall provides a hands-on analysis of 10 of the most frequently played tunes in the jazz genre, as played by the leading guitarists of all time. Features: All the Things You Are • How Insensitive • I'll Remember April • So What • Yesterdays • and more.
00695586 Book/CD Pack......................................$24.95

GUITAR STANDARDS

Classic Jazz Masters Series

16 classic jazz guitar performances transcribed note for note with tablature: All of You (Kenny Burrell) • Easter Parade (Herb Ellis) • I'll Remember April (Grant Green) • Lover Man (Django Reinhardt) • Song for My Father (George Benson) • The Way You Look Tonight (Wes Montgomery) • and more. Includes a discography.
00699143 Guitar Transcriptions $14.95

JAZZ CLASSICS

Jazz Guitar Chord Melody Solos
arr. Jeff Arnold

27 rich arrangements of jazz classics: Blue in Green • Bluesette • Doxy • Epistrophy • Footprints • Giant Steps • Lush Life • A Night in Tunisia • Nuages • St. Thomas • Waltz for Debby • Yardbird Suite • and more.
00699758 Solo Guitar $12.95

JAZZ CLASSICS FOR SOLO GUITAR

arranged by Robert B. Yelin

This collection includes excellent chord melody arrangements in standard notation and tablature for 35 all-time jazz favorites: April in Paris • Cry Me a River • Day by Day • God Bless' the Child • It Might as Well Be Spring • Lover • My Romance • Nuages • Satin Doll • Tenderly • Unchained Melody • Wave • and more!
00699279 Solo Guitar $17.95

JAZZ FAVORITES FOR SOLO GUITAR

arranged by Robert B. Yelin

This fantastic 35-song collection includes lush chord melody arrangements in standard notation and tab: Autumn in New York • Call Me Irresponsible • How Deep Is the Ocean • I Could Write a Book • The Lady Is a Tramp • Mood Indigo • Polka Dots and Moonbeams • Solitude • Take the "A" Train • Where or When • more.
00699278 Solo Guitar $17.95

JAZZ FOR THE ROCK GUITARIST

by Michael Mueller

Take your playing beyond barre chords and the blues box! This book/CD pack will take you through the essentials of the jazz idiom with plenty of exercises and examples – all of which are demonstrated on the accompanying CD.
00695856 Book/CD Pack......................................$14.95

JAZZ GEMS FOR SOLO GUITAR

arranged by Robert B. Yelin

35 great solo arrangements of jazz classics, including: After You've Gone • Alice in Wonderland • The Christmas Song • Four • Meditation • Stompin' at the Savoy • Sweet and Lovely • Waltz for Debby • Yardbird Suite • You'll Never Walk Alone • You've Changed • and more.
00699617 Solo Guitar $17.95

JAZZ GUITAR BIBLE

The one book that has all of the jazz guitar classics transcribed note-for-note, with standard notation and tablature. Includes over 30 songs: Body and Soul • Girl Talk • I'll Remember April • In a Sentimental Mood • My Funny Valentine • Nuages • Satin Doll • So What • Stardust • Take Five • Tangerine • Yardbird Suite • and more.
00690466 Guitar Recorded Versions $19.95

JAZZ GUITAR CHORD MELODIES

arranged & performed by Dan Towey

This book/CD pack includes complete solo performances of 12 standards, including: All the Things You Are • Body and Soul • My Romance • How Insensitive • My One and Only Love • and more. The arrangements are performance level and range in difficulty from intermediate to advanced.
00698988 Book/CD Pack $19.95

JAZZ GUITAR PLAY-ALONG

Guitar Play-Along Volume 16

With this book/CD pack, all you have to do is follow the tab, listen to the CD to hear how the guitar should sound, and then play along using the separate backing tracks. 8 songs: All Blues • Bluesette • Footprints • How Insensitive (Insensatez) • Misty • Satin Doll • Stella by Starlight • Tenor Madness.
00699584 Book/CD Pack $15.95

JAZZ STANDARDS FOR FINGERSTYLE GUITAR

20 songs, including: All the Things You Are • Autumn Leaves • Bluesette • Body and Soul • Fly Me to the Moon • The Girl from Ipanema • How Insensitive • I've Grown Accustomed to Her Face • My Funny Valentine • Satin Doll • Stompin' at the Savoy • and more.
00699029 Fingerstyle Guitar $10.95

JAZZ STANDARDS FOR SOLO GUITAR

arranged by Robert B. Yelin

35 chord melody guitar arrangements, including: Ain't Misbehavin' • Autumn Leaves • Bewitched • Cherokee • Darn That Dream • Girl Talk • I've Got You Under My Skin • Lullaby of Birdland • My Funny Valentine • A Nightingale Sang in Berkeley Square • Stella by Starlight • The Very Thought of You • and more.
00699277 Solo Guitar $17.95

101 MUST-KNOW JAZZ LICKS

by Wolf Marshall

Add a jazz feel and flavor to your playing! 101 definitive licks, plus a demonstration CD, from every major jazz guitar style, neatly organized into easy-to-use categories. They're all here: swing and pre-bop, bebop, post-bop modern jazz, hard bop and cool jazz, modal jazz, soul jazz and postmodern jazz.
00695433 Book/CD Pack.....................................$17.95

FOR MORE INFORMATION, SEE YOUR LOCAL MUSIC DEALER, OR WRITE TO:

HAL•LEONARD®
CORPORATION

7777 W. BLUEMOUND RD. P.O. BOX 13819 MILWAUKEE, WI 53213

Visit Hal Leonard Online at **www.halleonard.com**

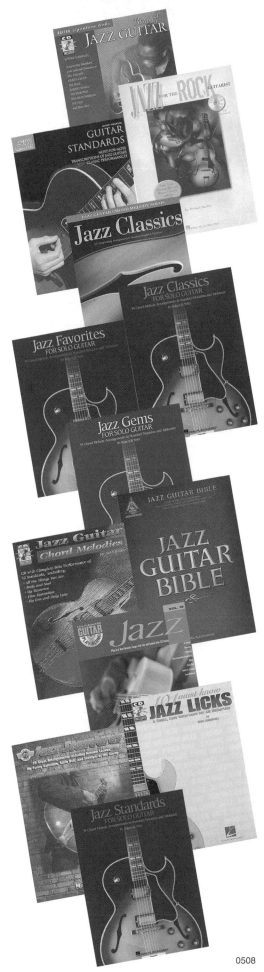

Prices, contents and availability subject to change without notice.

0508

· AUTHENTIC CHORDS · ORIGINAL KEYS · COMPLETE SONGS ·

The *Strum It* series lets players strum the chords and sing along with their favorite hits. Each song has been selected because it can be played with regular open chords, barre chords, or other moveable chord types. Guitarists can simply play the rhythm, or play and sing along through the entire song. All songs are shown in their original keys complete with chords, strum patterns, melody and lyrics. Wherever possible, the chord voicings from the recorded versions are notated.

Acoustic Classics   00699238 / $10.95
21 classics: And I Love Her • Barely Breathing • Free Fallin' • Maggie May • Mr. Jones • Only Wanna Be with You • Patience • Wonderful Tonight • Yesterday • more.

The Beach Boys'
Greatest Hits   00699357/ $12.95
19 tunes: Barbara Ann • California Girls • Fun, Fun Fun • Good Vibrations • Help Me Rhonda • I Get Around • Surfer Girl • Surfin' U.S.A. • Wouldn't It Be Nice • more.

The Beatles Favorites   00699249 / $14.95
23 Beatles hits: Can't Buy Me Love • Eight Days a Week • Hey Jude • Let It Be • She Loves You • Yesterday • You've Got to Hide Your Love Away • and more.

Best of Contemporary
Christian   00699531 / $12.95
20 CCM favorites: Awesome God • Butterfly Kisses • El Shaddai • Father's Eyes • I Could Sing of Your Love Forever • Jesus Freak • The Potter's Hand • and more.

Best of Steven
Curtis Chapman   00699530 / $12.95
16 top hits: For the Sake of the Call • Heaven in the Real World • His Strength Is Perfect • I Will Be Here • More to This Life • Signs of Life • What Kind of Joy • more.

Very Best of
Johnny Cash   00699514 / $10.95
17 songs: A Boy Named Sue • Daddy Sang Bass • Folsom Prison Blues • I Walk the Line • The Man in Black • Orange Blossom Special • Ring of Fire • and more.

Celtic Guitar Songbook   00699265 / $9.95
35 songs: Cockles and Mussels • Danny Boy • The Irish Washerwoman • Kerry Dance • Killarney • My Wild Irish Rose • Sailor's Hornpipe • and more.

Christmas Songs
for Guitar   00699247 / $10.95
40 favorites: Frosty the Snow Man • Grandma Got Run Over by a Reindeer • I'll Home for Christmas • Rockin' Around the Christmas Tree • Silver Bells • more.

Christmas Songs
with 3 Chords   00699487 / $8.95
30 all-time favorites: Angels We Have Heard on High • Away in a Manger • Here We Come A-Wassailing • Jolly Old St. Nicholas • Silent Night • Up on the Housetop • more.

Very Best of
Eric Clapton   00699560 / $12.95
20 songs: Change the World • For Your Love • I Shot the Sheriff • Layla • My Father's Eyes • Tears in Heaven • White Room • Wonderful Tonight • and more.

Country Strummin'   00699119 / $8.95
Features 24 songs: Achy Breaky Heart • Blue • A Broken Wing • Gone Country • I Fall to Pieces • She and I • Unchained Melody • What a Crying Shame • and more.

Jim Croce – Classic Hits   00699269 / $10.95
22 great songs: Bad, Bad Leroy Brown • I'll Have to Say I Love You in a Song • Operator (That's Not the Way It Feels) • Time in a Bottle • and more.

Very Best of
John Denver   00699488 / $12.95
20 top hits: Leaving on a Jet Plane • Rocky Mountain High • Sunshine on My Shoulders • Take Me Home, Country Roads • Thank God I'm a Country Boy • more.

Neil Diamond   00699593 / $12.95
28 classics: America • Cracklin' Rosie • Forever in Blue Jeans • Hello Again • I'm a Believer • Love on the Rocks • Song Sung Blue • Sweet Caroline • and more.

Disney Favorites   00699171 / $10.95
34 Disney favorites: Can You Feel the Love Tonight • Cruella De Vil • Friend Like Me • It's a Small World • Under the Sea • Whistle While You Work • and more.

Disney Greats   00699172 / $10.95
39 classics: Beauty and the Beast • Colors of the Wind • Go the Distance • Heigh-Ho • Kiss the Girl • When You Wish Upon a Star • Zip-A-Dee-Doo-Dah • and more.

Best of The Doors   00699177 / $10.95
25 Doors favorites: Been Down So Long • Hello I Love You Won't You Tell Me Your Name? • Light My Fire • Riders on the Storm • Touch Me • and more.

Favorite Songs
with 3 Chords   00699112 / $8.95
27 popular songs: All Shook Up • Boot Scootin' Boogie • Great Balls of Fire • Lay Down Sally • Semi-Charmed Life • Twist and Shout • Wooly Bully • and more.

Favorite Songs
with 4 Chords   00699270 / $8.95
22 tunes: Beast of Burden • Don't Be Cruel • Gloria • I Fought the Law • La Bamba • Last Kiss • Let Her Cry • Love Stinks • Peggy Sue • 3 AM • Wild Thing • and more.

Fireside Sing-Along   00699273 / $8.95
25 songs: Edelweiss • Leaving on a Jet Plane • Take Me Home, Country Roads • Teach Your Children • This Land Is Your Land • You've Got a Friend • and more.

Folk Favorites   00699517 / $8.95
42 traditional favorites: Camptown Races • Clementine • Danny Boy • My Old Kentucky Home • Rock-A-My Soul • Scarborough Fair • and more.

Irving Berlin's
God Bless America®   00699508 / $9.95
25 patriotic anthems: America, the Beautiful • Battle Hymn of the Republic • God Bless America • The Star Spangled Banner • This Land Is Your Land • and more.

Great '50s Rock   00699187 / $9.95
28 hits: At the Hop • Blueberry Hill • Bye Bye Love • Hound Dog • Rock Around the Clock • That'll Be the Day • and more.

Great '60s Rock   00699188 / $9.95
27 classic rock songs: And I Love Her • Gloria • Mellow Yellow • Return to Sender • Runaway • Surfin' U.S.A. • The Twist • Under the Boardwalk • Wild Thing • more.

Great '70s Rock   00699262 / $9.95
21 classic hits: Band on the Run • Lay Down Sally • Let It Be • Love Hurts • Ramblin' Man • Time for Me to Fly • Two Out of Three Ain't Bad • Wild World • and more.

Great '80s Rock   00699263 / $9.95
23 favorites: Centerfold • Free Fallin' • Got My Mind Set on You • Kokomo • Should I Stay or Should I Go • Uptown Girl • What I Like About You • and more.

Great '90s Rock   00699268 / $9.95
17 contemporary hits: If You Could Only See • Iris • Mr. Jones • Only Wanna Be with You • Tears in Heaven • Torn • The Way • You Were Meant for Me • and more.

Best of Woody Guthrie   00699496 / $12.95
20 songs: Do Re Mi • The Grand Coulee Dam • Roll On, Columbia • So Long It's Been Good to Know Yuh • This Land Is Your Land • Tom Joad • and more.

John Hiatt Collection   00699398 / $12.95
17 classics: Angel Eyes • Feels Like Rain • Have a Little Faith in Me • Riding with the King • Thing Called Love (Are You Ready for This Thing Called Love) • and more.

Hymn Favorites   00699271 / $9.95
Includes: Amazing Grace • Down by the Riverside • Holy, Holy, Holy • Just as I Am • Rock of Ages • What a Friend We Have in Jesus • and more.

Carole King Collection   00699234 / $12.95
20 songs: I Feel the Earth Move • It's Too Late • A Natural Woman • So Far Away • Tapestry • Will You Love Me Tomorrow • You've Got a Friend • and more.

Very Best of
Dave Matthews Band   00699520 / $12.95
12 favorites: Ants Marching • Crash into Me • Crush • Don't Drink the Water • Everyday • The Space Between • Stay (Wasting Time) • What Would You Say • and more.

Sarah McLachlan   00699231 / $10.95
20 of Sarah's hits: Angel • Building a Mystery • I Will Remember You • Ice Cream • Sweet Surrender • more.

A Merry
Christmas Songbook   00699211 / $8.95
51 holiday hits: Away in a Manger • Deck the Hall • Fum, Fum, Fum • The Holly and the Ivy • Jolly Old St. Nicholas • O Christmas Tree • and more!

More Favorite Songs
with 3 Chords   00699532 / $8.95
27 great hits: Barbara Ann • Gloria • Hang on Sloopy • Hound Dog • La Bamba • Mony, Mony • Rock Around the Clock • Rock This Town • Rockin' Robin • and more.

The Very Best of
Tom Petty   00699366 / $12.95
16 favorites: American Girl • Breakdown • Free Fallin' • Here Comes My Girl • Into the Great Wide Open • Learning to Fly • Runnin' Down a Dream • and more.

Pop-Rock
Guitar Favorites   00699088 / $8.95
31 songs: Angie • Brown Eyed Girl • Eight Days a Week • Free Bird • Gloria • Hey Jude • Let It Be • Maggie May • Wild Thing • Wonderful Tonight • and more.

Elvis! Greatest Hits   00699276 / $10.95
24 Elvis classics: All Shook Up • Always on My Mind • Can't Help Falling in Love • Hound Dog • It's Now or Never • Jailhouse Rock • Love Me Tender • and more.

Songs for Kids   00699616 / $9.95
28 fun favorites: Alphabet Song • Bingo • Frere Jacques • Kum Ba Yah • London Bridge • Old MacDonald • Pop Goes the Weasel • Yankee Doodle • more.

Best of George Strait   00699235 / $10.95
20 Strait hits: Adalida • All My Ex's Live in Texas • Carried Away • Does Fort Worth Ever Cross Your Mind • Right or Wrong • Write This Down • and more.

Best of
Hank Williams Jr.   00699224 / $12.95
24 signature standards: All My Rowdy Friends Are Coming Over Tonight • Honky Tonkin' • There's a Tear in My Beer • Whiskey Bent and Hell Bound • and more.

Women of Rock   00699183 / $9.95
22 hits: Don't Speak • Give Me One Reason • I Don't Want to Wait • Insensitive • Lovefool • Stay • Torn • You Oughta Know • You Were Meant for Me • and more.

FOR MORE INFORMATION, SEE YOUR LOCAL MUSIC DEALER,
OR WRITE TO:

7777 W. BLUEMOUND RD. P.O. BOX 13819 MILWAUKEE, WI 53213

Visit Hal Leonard online at **www.halleonard.com**

Prices, contents & availability subject to change without notice.

1008